Detroit Public Library

Understanding your
Muscles
& Bones

The muscles that made this book belong to:

Rebecca Treays who wrote the words
Christyan Fox who drew the pictures
Revd Dr Michael Reiss, the muscles and bones expert

Martin Aggett who did the designs

CHANEY BRANCH LIBRARY
16101 GRAND RIVER
DETROIT, MI 48227
APR - - 2007

INTRODUCTION

CONTENTS

2 Introduction

4 Your skeleton

6 Skeletal muscles

8 Joints

10 Moving parts

12 Looking inside

14 Your heart

16 Body batteries

18 Strength and sports

20 Involuntary muscles

22 Muscle talk

24 Growing

26 Broken bones

28 Muscle trouble

30 Prehistoric bones

31 Amazing facts

32 Index

Your muscles and bones work together as a team allowing you to run, jump, skip, play sports or just turn on the TV. Without them you would just be a soggy heap of body matter, doomed to live out your life as a motionless blob.

Look at your hands. Think of all the different things you can do with them, from gripping tightly to playing the violin.

It is an intricate system of muscles and bones which gives you this flexibility.

This shows the muscles in your hand.

Food for Thought

If you eat meat you are actually eating animal muscle.

BRAIN POWER

Your muscles can only move under instructions from your brain. Your ability and skill at controlling your movement is called coordination.

Tiny babies' movements are very limited as they have no coordination.

A toddler's brain is just beginning to develop coordination.

Soccer players have to coordinate many parts of their bodies to hit a ball on target.

CELLS AND TISSUES

Bone tissue

Muscle and bone are types of body tissues. Tissue is made up of cells. Cells are the building blocks of your body. Bone tissue is made up of bone cells. Muscle tissue is made up of muscle cells. There are several types of muscle tissue. You will find out about them all in this book.

EXPERTS

Some doctors and scientists are experts in muscles and bones.

Osteologists study the structure and function of bones.

Physiotherapists try to rebuild your muscles if they have been weakened by disease or an accident.

Osteopaths try to heal many illnesses by massaging and moving muscles and bones.

Finger Facts

There are 27 bones and 37 muscles in your hand.

Each finger contains three bones and each thumb two. This allows you to curve them around a pen to write.

Did you hear the one about the skeleton who wouldn't do his homework? He was bone idle!

YOUR SKELETON

Your skeleton is a frame which gives shape to all the soft jelly-like parts of your body and stops them from falling in a flaccid heap on the floor. It also forms a protective cage around your organs, such as your heart, and prevents them from getting damaged by knocks and bumps.

You might expect adults to have more bones than babies, but actually it is the other way around. There are 206 bones in a fully-grown human skeleton, but more than 300 in a baby's. This is because, as we grow, some of our bones fuse together to form bigger bones.

Nearly half of all your bones are in your hands and feet.

Distal phalanx
Middle phalanx
Proximal phalanx
Metacarpal

Carpus

Your skull is like a crash helmet protecting your brain.

Bone from your ear

The smallest bone in your body is only 3mm (0.12in) long. It is found in your ear and it vibrates to let you hear.

An adult skeleton

Skull

Humerus

Sternum (breast bone)

NECKTIES

Your neck contains seven vertebrae. How many do you think a giraffe has? (Answer on page 31.)

Clavicle (collar bone)

Ulna
Radius

Scapula (shoulder blade)

12 ribs form a cage to protect your lungs and heart.

Vertebral column (spine or backbone) made up of 33 vertebrae

SPINES, SHELLS AND BODY BAGS

Humans are vertebrates. This means we have a backbone, or spine. Your spine is your body's main support. Some other vertebrates share the same type of skeleton as humans. So although you look totally different from a pig, cat or rabbit, your skeleton follows the same general pattern as theirs, with a skull, four limbs and a spine.

Bird skeleton

Fish and birds are vertebrates too, but their skeletons follow a different pattern.

Cat skeleton

Animals without spines are called invertebrates. Some invertebrates, such as crabs, have an exoskeleton - a hard shell-like skeleton outside their bodies.

Crab

Other, simpler animals, such as worms, have no skeleton. All their body parts are contained in a bag.

Earthworm

Femur - the biggest bone in the body

Ilium

Sacrum   *Ischium*

Pubis

Patella (knee cap)

Coccyx. Some scientists think your coccyx is all that remains of a tail which disappeared as humans evolved.

Tibia

Fibula

Middle phalanx

Distal phalanx

Proximal phalanx

Metatarsal

Tarsus

SKELETAL MUSCLES

Each person has about 600 muscles, called skeletal muscles, attached to their skeleton. They keep the skeleton upright and give your bones the power to move. Skeletal muscles are also called voluntary muscles. This is because you can consciously control their movement. Skeletal muscles have Latin names, which are used and understood by scientists all over the world.

MUSCLE FUEL

In order to work, muscles need a gas called oxygen. Oxygen is carried around your body by your blood. The harder your muscles work, the more oxygen they need. When you start to run, more blood is sent to your leg muscles. If the blood can't get there quickly enough, your muscles don't get enough oxygen so they begin to ache. This is called muscle fatigue.

This picture shows the main muscles attached to the skeleton.

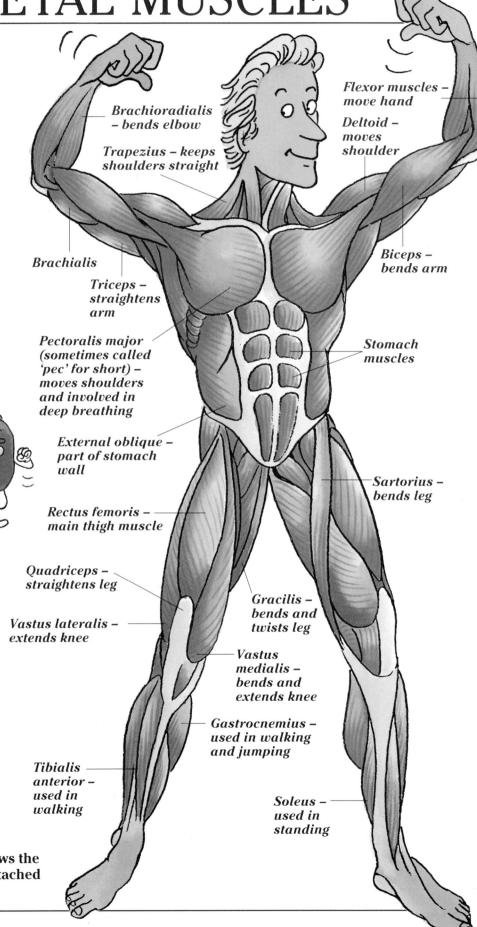

Brachioradialis – bends elbow

Trapezius – keeps shoulders straight

Flexor muscles – move hand

Deltoid – moves shoulder

Brachialis

Biceps – bends arm

Triceps – straightens arm

Pectoralis major (sometimes called 'pec' for short) – moves shoulders and involved in deep breathing

Stomach muscles

External oblique – part of stomach wall

Sartorius – bends leg

Rectus femoris – main thigh muscle

Quadriceps – straightens leg

Gracilis – bends and twists leg

Vastus lateralis – extends knee

Vastus medialis – bends and extends knee

Gastrocnemius – used in walking and jumping

Tibialis anterior – used in walking

Soleus – used in standing

MAKING FACES

You have over 40 muscles in your face - more than any other animal. This makes you very expressive. You can communicate many emotions through your facial expressions. Can you tell what these people are feeling just by looking at their faces?

CLENCH TEST

Hold your hand above your head, and see how many times you can clench and unclench your fist before it begins to ache. Once the aching has stopped, try the same thing with your other hand down by your side.

You should be able to manage more clenches with your hand hanging down because it is easier for blood to flow down into your hand rather than upward.

TALES OF CLASSIC TENDONS

Muscles are attached to bones by tough, inelastic (non-stretchy) bands called tendons. The tendon which attaches the muscle to the back of your foot is easily damaged during exercise. It is called the Achilles tendon, after an ancient Greek story (see below). The expression "Achilles heel" is also used to describe any weakness in an otherwise strong person.

Achilles tendon

1. Thetis dipped her baby son Achilles in a sacred river to protect him from danger.

2. The only spot which stayed dry was his heel. This became his weak spot.

3. Achilles was eventually killed by an arrow wound in his heel.

JOINTS

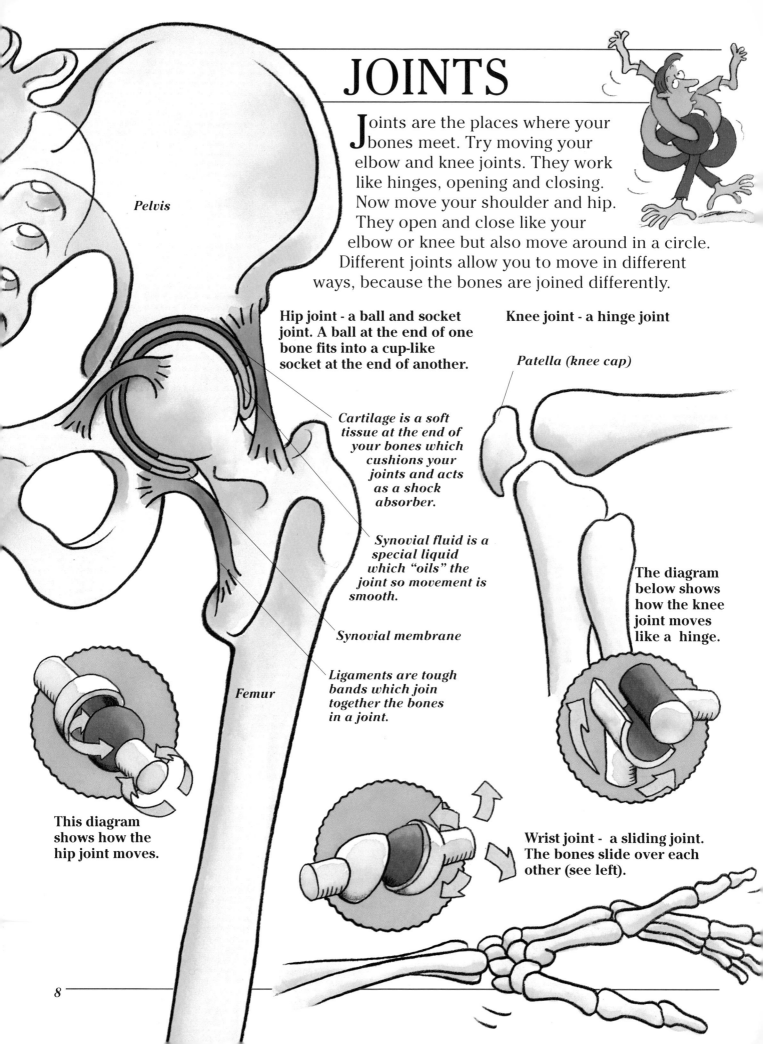

Joints are the places where your bones meet. Try moving your elbow and knee joints. They work like hinges, opening and closing. Now move your shoulder and hip. They open and close like your elbow or knee but also move around in a circle. Different joints allow you to move in different ways, because the bones are joined differently.

Pelvis

Hip joint - a ball and socket joint. A ball at the end of one bone fits into a cup-like socket at the end of another.

Knee joint - a hinge joint

Patella (knee cap)

Cartilage is a soft tissue at the end of your bones which cushions your joints and acts as a shock absorber.

Synovial fluid is a special liquid which "oils" the joint so movement is smooth.

Synovial membrane

The diagram below shows how the knee joint moves like a hinge.

Ligaments are tough bands which join together the bones in a joint.

Femur

This diagram shows how the hip joint moves.

Wrist joint - a sliding joint. The bones slide over each other (see left).

CREAKY JOINTS

Joints are one of your body's trouble spots. They are under almost constant pressure and tend, especially as you grow older, to develop faults.

It is easy to sprain a wrist or ankle. Sprains happen if you twist a joint suddenly and tear or snap the tendon or ligament. Sprains can be painful, but they usually heal themselves given time and rest.

Arthritis is a disease which causes joints to swell up so they become difficult to move. There are two kinds of arthritis.

In osteoarthritis, the cartilage in the joints wears down. So instead of moving smoothly, the bones grind against each other.

In rheumatoid arthritis, the bones in the joint become fused together. This makes any movement impossible.

Osteoarthritis usually happens in older people, but people of any age can get rheumatoid arthritis.

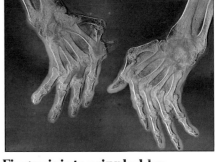

Finger joints crippled by rheumatoid arthritis

Joints are not designed to withstand the vigorous training that some sports demand. When a joint is used too much, its lining can get inflamed and it can produce too much synovial fluid (see opposite).

I think I've got Tennis Elbow.

You're just highly strung.

People who use their arms a lot, such as tennis players, can suffer from "tennis elbow" - an inflamed elbow caused by overuse.

SPLITS AND BACK FLIPS

Gymnasts and acrobats can bend their bodies into shapes which could put any normal person in the hospital! This is because they are very supple. This means they have more movement in their joints. You can become supple by doing special exercises which stretch your body beyond its normal range. These must only be done with a trained instructor, or you could hurt yourself badly.

MOVING PARTS

Every time you move, your brain, nerves, muscles and bones all work together in a highly complex way. Your brain receives information from your senses. This is evaluated and a decision is made about whether the body should move in response. If movement is needed, messages, called impulses, are sent down nerve cells, usually via your spinal cord, to nerve endings at your muscles. The nerve endings stimulate the muscles into action and you move.

1. Information from the senses (in this case the eyes) is sent to the brain.

2. The brain decides what response is needed.

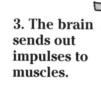

3. The brain sends out impulses to muscles.

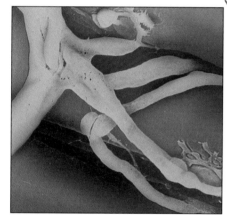

This photograph shows a magnified image of nerve endings (in yellow) meeting a muscle (in pink).

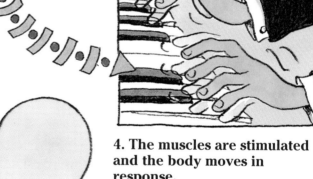

4. The muscles are stimulated and the body moves in response.

PAIRS

Muscles move bones by contracting. When a muscle contracts, it tightens and shortens, pulling a bone with it. But muscles can't push. This means they have to work in pairs: one to pull a bone one way, and the other to pull it back again.

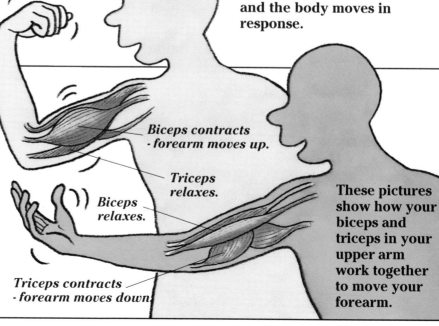

Biceps contracts - forearm moves up.

Triceps relaxes.

Biceps relaxes.

Triceps contracts - forearm moves down.

These pictures show how your biceps and triceps in your upper arm work together to move your forearm.

LEONARDO

In Europe, between five and six hundred years ago, people became very interested in the human body and how it worked. Artists, such as Leonardo da Vinci, studied the body and muscles in particular. Leonardo filled many sketch books with his drawings of the structure of muscles.

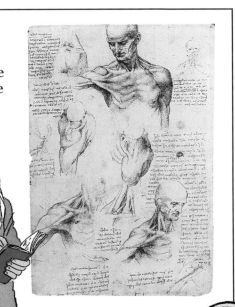

RUMBLING THUMBS

Put both thumbs gently into your ears and then clench your fists. As you clench you should hear a rumbling sound. This is the sound of your muscles vibrating as they contract. The tighter you clench, the more your muscles contract and the louder the rumbling sounds will become.

REFLEX ACTIONS

Actions such as dancing or pressing a doorbell are voluntary. This means they are the result of a conscious decision. But there are some actions which are involuntary, over which you have no control. One special kind of involuntary action is a reflex action.

A reflex action is your body's response to a dangerous situation. It happens so quickly you are not aware of what your body has done until the action is over. This is because the message to act comes from the spinal cord and not your brain. The brain is only told what has gone on after it has happened.

This diagram shows you what happens when you step on a spike and a reflex action takes place.

❶ Sharp spike touches pain receptors in your foot.

❷ Nerve endings send information to special nerve cells in the spinal cord. The brain is bypassed.

❸ The spinal cord processes this information and sends impulses down to the muscle that moves your leg. The brain is also sent impulses informing it of the action.

❹ Leg moves.

LOOKING INSIDE

Bone might look dead, but it is in fact very much alive. Bone is a living tissue made up of bone cells, blood vessels and nerves. Bone can grow, repair itself and hurt if it is damaged.

WHAT MAKES BONES STRONG?

Compact bone is the hard, strong part of your bones. It is made strong by a mineral called calcium. We get calcium from the food we eat. It is very important for babies to drink a lot of milk, because it contains the calcium that will make their bones harden. Calcium also makes your teeth hard.

Inside a bone

The outer part of the bone is called compact bone. This is the hard part.

In the middle of the bone is a tube containing a jelly called marrow.

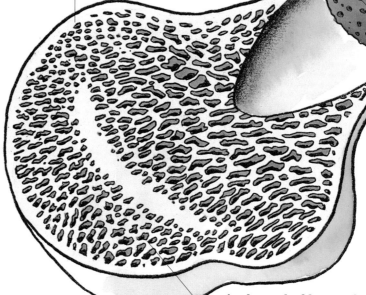

At the end of bones, beneath the compact bone, is a lighter substance called spongy bone. It isn't spongy to touch, but it does look a little like sponge.

BENDING BONES

Take a chicken leg bone and put it in a bowl filled with vinegar. Leave it for two to three days.

Pour away the vinegar, wash the bone with water and then try to bend it.

The bone bends because the vinegar has dissolved the calcium in it.

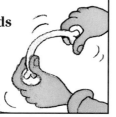

BLOOD FACTORY

In the marrow of a few bones, over two million new blood cells are being made every second. This is a vital task, essential for your survival.

You have two types of blood cells: red and white. Red blood cells carry essential substances around your body. White blood cells are germ-busters. They defend against disease. There are two main types of white blood cells: phagocytes and lymphocytes. Phagocytes kill germ cells by eating

Yummy!

Phagocyte

FRRZZZT!

TAKE THAT GERMS!

FRRZZZT!

Lymphocyte

them. Lymphocytes kill germs by blasting them with chemicals called antibodies.

OLD BONES

This human skeleton is over 1500 years old. The rest of the body would have decomposed soon after the person died.

The bones in the skeleton above are not alive like yours. The bone cells have died and all that is left is calcium and other minerals. They would crumble if handled roughly.

This was obviously a left handed vegetarian who enjoyed football and...

Archeologists can find out a lot about how people lived by looking at old bones. By testing the minerals in skeletons, they can figure out what people ate. From this they may be able to suggest whether they were hunters or farmers, and so what tools and weapons they made.

MUSCLE TISSUE

Muscles are made of muscle tissue. There are three different types of muscle tissue: heart muscle, smooth muscle and striped muscle. Heart muscle makes up your heart. Smooth muscle makes up the muscles in the walls of your gut and other organs. Striped muscle makes up your skeletal muscles.

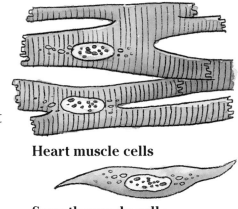

Heart muscle cells

Smooth muscle cell

Striped muscle consists of bundles of cords. Each cord is made up of two kinds of strands, or filaments. Muscles contract when these filaments overlap and lock into each other.

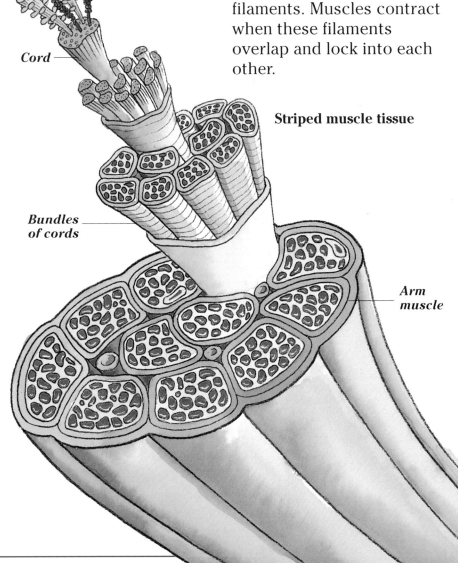

Filament

Cord

Striped muscle tissue

Bundles of cords

Arm muscle

YOUR HEART

Your heart is an amazingly efficient muscle. It never stops working and it never gets tired. It is the life force of your body, pumping blood to all corners of your body.

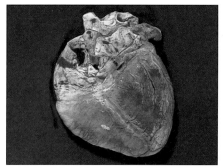

Photograph of a human heart

HEART BEATS

If you put your hand on your chest you can feel your heart beating. Each beat is caused by your heart muscle contracting (tightening) and then relaxing. This happens about 100,000 times a day or about 70 times a minute.

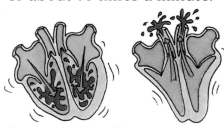

Heart relaxes   Heart contracts

When your heart is relaxed, blood flows into it from the veins. When it contracts, blood is pumped out of the heart into the arteries. If your body is working very hard it needs more blood, so your heart beats faster.

Your heart is divided into two halves: right and left. Each half is made up of an upper "chamber" called an atrium and a lower "chamber" called a ventricle.

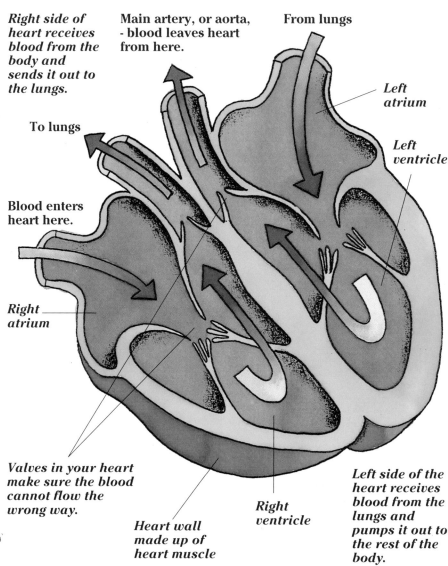

Right side of heart receives blood from the body and sends it out to the lungs.

To lungs

Blood enters heart here.

Right atrium

Valves in your heart make sure the blood cannot flow the wrong way.

Main artery, or aorta, - blood leaves heart from here.

From lungs

Left atrium

Left ventricle

Heart wall made up of heart muscle

Right ventricle

Left side of the heart receives blood from the lungs and pumps it out to the rest of the body.

LOVEHEARTS

Many people think that their emotions come from their heart, but this is nonsense. It is your brain that allows you to fall in love or get upset. Feeling something strongly does however often make your heart beat faster. This is because when you get excited your body works harder and so your heart needs to pump more blood.

BLOOD FLOW

Your body contains about a small bucketful of blood. Blood is used to transport things around your body. It circulates endlessly, delivering oxygen, food and chemicals wherever they are needed. It also picks up poisonous waste and carries it to where it can be dealt with safely.

Your blood is transported in thin tubes called blood vessels. There are three types of blood vessels: arteries, veins and capillaries. Arteries carry blood away from the heart, veins carry blood to the heart, and capillaries join arteries to veins.

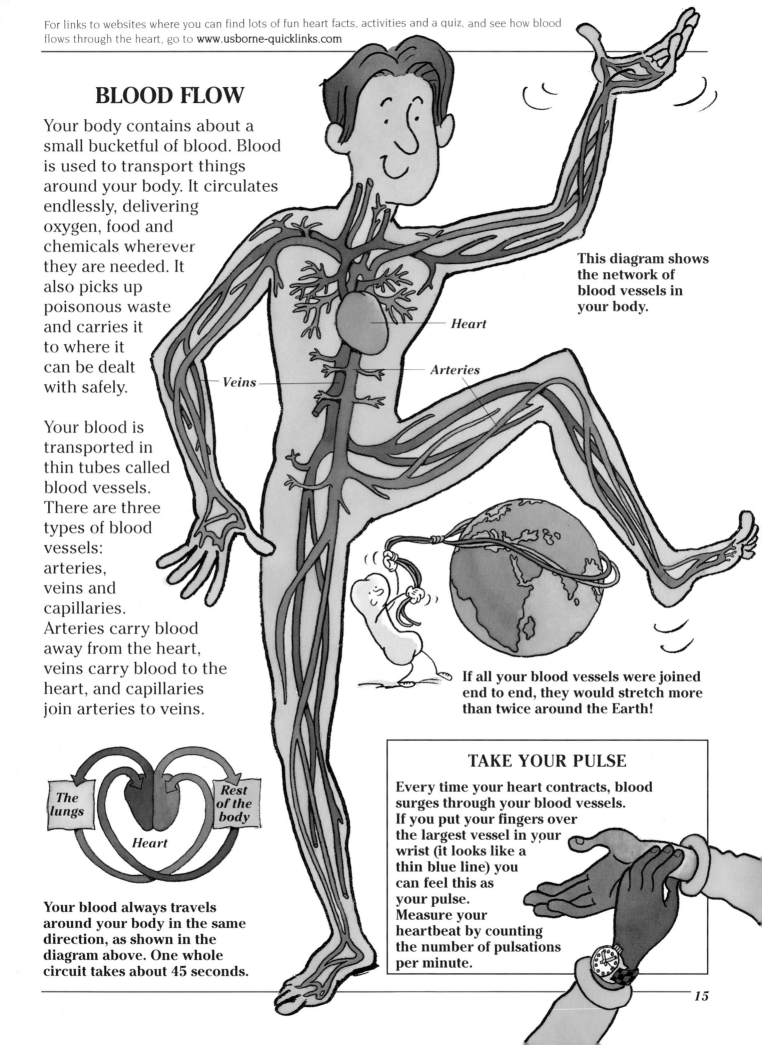

Veins

Heart

Arteries

This diagram shows the network of blood vessels in your body.

If all your blood vessels were joined end to end, they would stretch more than twice around the Earth!

The lungs

Rest of the body

Heart

Your blood always travels around your body in the same direction, as shown in the diagram above. One whole circuit takes about 45 seconds.

TAKE YOUR PULSE

Every time your heart contracts, blood surges through your blood vessels. If you put your fingers over the largest vessel in your wrist (it looks like a thin blue line) you can feel this as your pulse. Measure your heartbeat by counting the number of pulsations per minute.

BODY BATTERIES

Inside all your muscles is a vital substance called ATP. ATP is like a battery that stores energy. Your muscles can only contract if they have a constant supply of ATP. This is provided by a process called respiration. The more energetic you are, the more ATP you need. Without it your muscles are useless.

The lungs - vital for respiration

ATP AND OXYGEN

During respiration, food, which your body converts into a sort of sugar, is broken down in your muscle cells.

There are two types of respiration: aerobic and anaerobic. Aerobic means 'with oxygen'. During aerobic respiration, food reacts with oxygen to produce ATP. Your muscles get the oxygen they need for aerobic respiration from the air you breathe into your lungs.

When you breathe in, millions of air sacs in your lungs fill with air. Each of these air sacs is surrounded by masses of tiny blood vessels.

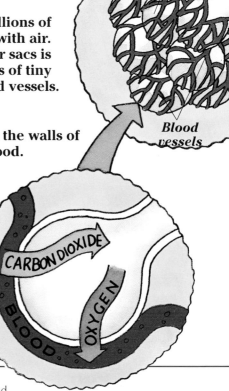

Air sacs

Blood vessels

Oxygen passes through the walls of the sacs into your blood. Carbon dioxide passes from the blood back into the lungs. It is then breathed out.

In aerobic respiration, oxygen and sugar react together. After some popping and fizzing, ATP, water and carbon dioxide are produced.

Once the oxygen is in your blood, it is pumped to your muscles by your heart.

For links to websites where you can watch a cartoon movie about lungs and find out more about how lungs work, go to **www.usborne-quicklinks.com**

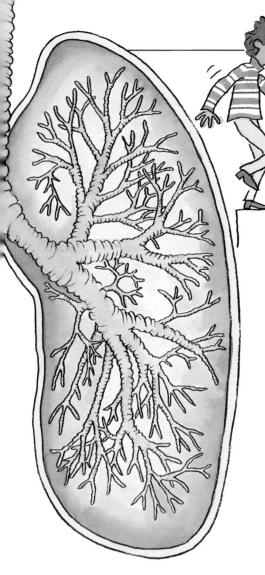

READY, STEADY, GO

Your heart can easily pump enough oxygen to your muscles to provide the energy you need for the less strenuous activities of everyday life, such as climbing upstairs. If you start dancing or skipping, your heart should still be able to supply enough oxygen for aerobic respiration. By beating faster it can get more oxygen to your muscles more quickly. But if you exercise really intensely, your heart won't be able to keep up. Then the anaerobic system takes over and ATP is produced without oxygen. The problem with anaerobic respiration is that it also produces a poison, called lactic acid. If lactic acid builds up in your muscles, it can give you muscle fatigue and stop you from moving altogether.

Anaerobic respiration is most useful when you need a lot of energy very quickly for a short amount of time: for example, for sprinting.

If you were running a mini-marathon, you would also need a lot of energy, but supplied more steadily, over a long period of time. For this you couldn't rely on anaerobic respiration, because the lactic acid would soon paralyze your muscles. Because of this, long-distance runners do special aerobic training to make their aerobic system more effective.

Aerobics is a popular form of aerobic training.

Aerobic training increases the oxygen in the blood and makes the heart beat stronger. Aerobic training must be hard, but not exhausting, and must be kept up regularly.

ENERGETIC ANIMALS

During respiration, some energy is released as heat. This is why you get hot when you exercise.

Other animals produce additional forms of energy. Some eels, for example, produce electricity. Glowworms produce light.

STRENGTH AND SPORTS

The more you use your muscles, the bigger they grow. And the bigger they grow, the stronger you will become. Strength is a very important part of many sports, and training to become stronger is vital in the preparation of any athlete.

TYPES OF STRENGTH

Strength is the ability of your muscles to exert a force on something to make it move. Strength always involves overcoming another force which doesn't want to move (either your own body or another object). This force is called resistance.

Force

Resistance

Different activities in sports require different types of strength.

General strength is the strength of all your muscles and how well they work together as a system. All sportsmen and women must have a good level of general strength.

Maximum strength is the greatest force which one muscle can exert.

Specific strength is the ability of particular muscles to perform a specific type of movement.

These athletes have a lot of specific strength in their arms.

Explosive strength is the ability of muscles to contract very quickly.

You use explosive strength to jump, throw and sprint.

Long distance running requires a lot of endurance.

Strength endurance is the ability to exert a force over a long period of time.

QUIZ

Which types of strength are most important in these activities? Answers on page 31.

1. Weight lifting

2. Competition to see who can do the most push-ups.

3. 100m sprint

BASIC TRAINING

Any training to make you stronger must follow three basic rules.

1. Muscles must be made to contract against a greater resistance than they are used to.

2. Resistance must be increased as training continues.

3. If training for a particular sport, the correct muscles must be exercised. If you want to be a runner, there is no point in doing hundreds of arm exercises.

Increase in muscle strength isn't permanent. If training is stopped, Mr. Powerhouse will eventually become Mr. Puny. The good news is that it takes about three times as long to lose new muscle strength as it does to gain it.

STRENGTH FROM STRESS

1. Exercise

2. Stress

3. Recovery

4. Stronger muscles

How does exercise make your muscles bigger? The answer is that it doesn't. It is the process of recovery from exercise that actually makes your muscles grow.

When you are training, two things are happening. First, your muscles are contracting more. Second, more chemical reactions are taking place in the muscle cells (see page 16). These two things put the body under stress, and it is the steps that are taken to stop this stress that make the muscle stronger.

Muscles don't actually start to get bigger until 24 to 48 hours after training has ended. Then individual muscle filaments begin to grow in thickness, so they can contract more strongly.

GREEK GOLDS

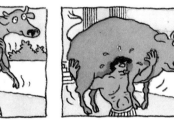

The Ancient Greek athlete, Milo of Cortona, used to lift a particular calf above his head daily. As the calf grew older and heavier, the resistance increased and

Milo's muscles grew stronger. Milo went on to win the top prize at six Olympic Games. This is one of the earliest examples of really effective training.

19

INVOLUNTARY MUSCLES

If you had to take care of the working of all your muscles all the time, you wouldn't have time to do anything else. Luckily, a part of your brain can control a whole host of muscles, without you being aware of it. These muscles are called involuntary muscles. You can take over control of some involuntary muscles when you need to.

DIGESTIVE MUSCLES

Your digestive system turns the food you eat into substances that can be absorbed into your blood. Involuntary muscles play a vital role in this process.

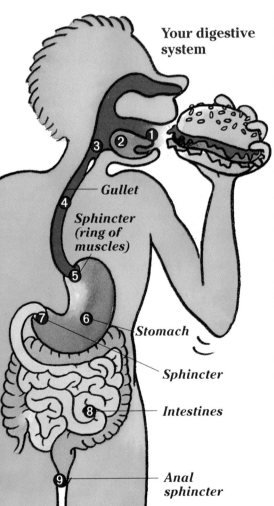

Your digestive system

Gullet

Sphincter (ring of muscles)

Stomach

Sphincter

Intestines

Anal sphincter

❶ Food is put into mouth.

❷ Food is chewed and shaped into a ball, or bolus, by tongue.

❸ Throat muscles open and you swallow. Bolus enters gullet.

❹ Bolus is pushed along by muscles in the gullet by a process called peristalsis.

Peristalsis

Muscles contract.   *Food moves.*

❺ Sphincter muscle at entrance to stomach relaxes (opens) so food enters stomach.

❻ Stomach muscles contract and relax. This churns food, mixing it with chemicals that break it down.

❼ Sphincter muscle at stomach's exit relaxes (opens) and food enters intestines.

❽ Food is pushed along by peristalsis. Digested food is absorbed into blood stream.

❾ Unwanted food is pushed out through the anal sphincter when you go to the toilet.

Which of these stages are usually controlled by involuntary muscles? (Answer on page 31.)

BREATHING

When you breathe, muscles force air in and out of your lungs. This is usually involuntary, but you can control your breathing if you want to.

Breathing in

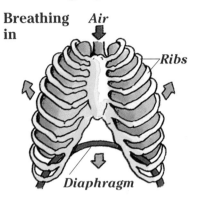

Air

Ribs

Diaphragm

1. An arched sheet of muscle under the lungs, called the diaphragm, contracts and flattens.

2. Muscles between the ribs contract, pulling the ribs up and out.

3. The lungs expand so air rushes into them to fill the space.

Breathing out

Air

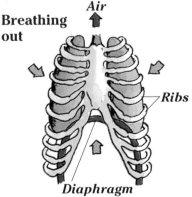

Ribs

Diaphragm

1. The diaphragm relaxes, so becomes arched again.

2. Rib muscles relax so the ribs move down and in.

3. Air is squeezed out of the lungs.

MUSCLE VISION

Seeing is a very complex process. Light rays travel into your eye through a tiny hole in the middle of your eye, called the pupil. The rays then pass through a lens which focuses them so they form a clear upside-down image on your retina (see below). This image is converted into nerve impulses. These impulses are sent to your brain, where they are interpreted as upright three-dimensional pictures. Without the work of involuntary muscles this process would not be possible.

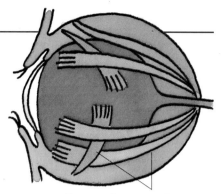

Eye socket muscles attach eyeball to skull.

You can't feel it, but these involuntary muscles make your eyeballs flicker constantly in your eye socket. You can take over control when you want.

This diagram shows a side view of the inside of an eye.

Pupil – hole through which light enters your eye. It looks like a black dot. It gets bigger in the dark and shrinks in the light.

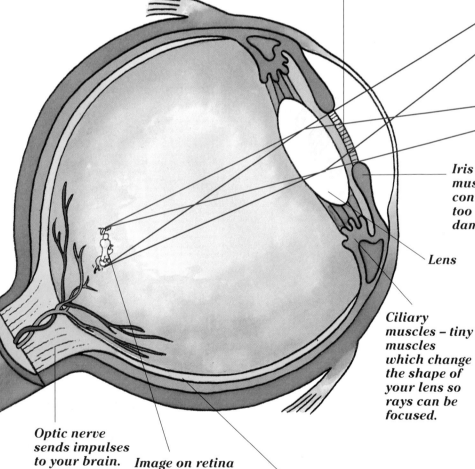

Light rays

Iris (tinted part of your eye) – a ring of muscle which opens and closes to control the size of your pupil. It stops too much light from getting in and damaging your eye.

Lens

Ciliary muscles – tiny muscles which change the shape of your lens so rays can be focused.

Optic nerve sends impulses to your brain.   *Image on retina*

Retina – layer of tissue at the back of your eyeball which contains millions of nerve cells.

DIM PUPILS

Stand in front of a mirror in a dimly lit room. Note the size of your pupils.

Shine a light into your face.

You should be able to see your pupils shrinking.

MUSCLE TALK

Y ou can speak. Speech is a series of different sounds with meanings. Human speech is very complicated and sets us apart from all other animals. In order to speak, you have to be able to control a system of different muscles.

WINDBAGS

In order to make any sound at all, you first have to have a stream of air. When you speak, you use the air you breathe out of your lungs. (You can use the air you breathe in, but it will be muffled and croaky. Try it and listen.)

Actors have special training to help them control their breathing.

Breathing is controlled by the plate of muscle under your lungs called the diaphragm.

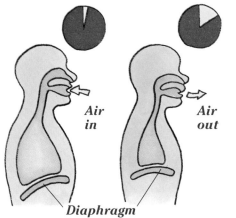

Breathe in for 2½ seconds.

Breathe out for 5-10 seconds.

Air in

Air out

Diaphragm

Usually you spend the same amount of time breathing in as you do breathing out - about 2½ seconds. But when you speak, you use your diaphragm to make the breathing out time last about 5-10 seconds. This means you can get more speaking time out of each breath.

VIBRATING VOICE BOX

When air leaves your lungs, it enters your voice box, or larynx (see diagram on page 23). Within your voice box are two muscly bands called vocal cords. These open and close rapidly, making the air in your voice box vibrate. These vibrations can be heard as sounds. The faster your vocal cords open and close, the higher the sound you will make. Women's vocal cords

open and close about 220 times a second, and men's about 120 times a second. This is why men have deeper voices.

View of vocal cords from above

Open

Closed

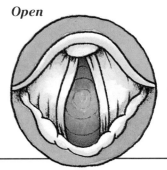

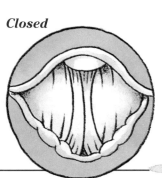

Sopranos (female singers) sing very high notes. Their vocal cords open and close up to 1000 times a second.

OOH, AHH, MUSCULAR

Air passes from your voice box into your vocal tract (see diagram on right). From here it leaves your body through your mouth or nose. On its way out, the air is affected by several muscles which work together to produce a wide range of speech sounds.

Say these words and see how the position of your lips changes:

cut

cat

curt

cool

Your lips are a ring of muscly tissue. You form them into different shapes for different sounds. They are completely closed for b, p and m sounds, and open different amounts for all the vowel sounds.

Your tongue is an incredibly flexible muscle, which can bend and curl into many different positions. It is vital for making nearly all speech sounds.

To see how important your tongue is, try to read this sentence out loud while holding down your tongue with your finger.

urmm yuurm thith... wuuth...

Your soft palate is a band of muscle at the back of your mouth. You can move it up and down to control how the air leaves your body. When it is up, air can escape only through your mouth. It is up for most sounds. When it is lowered, air can escape through your nose too. It is like this for nasal sounds, such as m, n and the 'oi' sound in 'oink'.

This diagram shows the main parts of your body involved in speech.

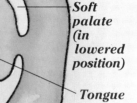

- Nasal cavity
- Lips
- Soft palate (in lowered position)
- Tongue
- Vocal tract
- Vocal cords
- Voice box (larynx)

TONGUE TWISTERS

Tongue twisters are phrases which are difficult to say clearly and quickly.

Try to say these tongue twisters over and over again, as fast as you can.

"Red lorry, yellow lorry"

"Peggy Babcock, Peggy Babcock"

GROWING

As you get older you grow taller because your bones get longer. The bones that grow the most are your leg bones - the femur, tibia and fibula. Most people have stopped growing by their early twenties. Some aren't happy with their final height and want to be taller or shorter. But once you have stopped growing, there is nothing you can do to change it.

BOUNCING BABES

Before it is born, a baby develops a skeleton. This skeleton is not made of bone, but of softer, gristly stuff called cartilage. (This is the same as the cartilage which cushions your joints.) After the baby is born, the cartilage slowly begins to turn into bone. This process is called ossification. By about the age of 12 nearly all your skeleton will be ossified.

A baby's cartilage skeleton makes it more flexible than older children and adults. They are less likely to break their bones.

GROWTH PLATES

Your bones cannot grow longer simply by making new bone cells. First they have to make new cartilage which is then turned into bone. Once your skeleton has ossified, some bones keep two small pads of cartilage. These are special growth plates (see right), which allow you to continue growing. In each plate the inner edge of the cartilage is gradually ossified. At the same time new cartilage grows at the outer edge. When growing stops completely, these plates of cartilage finally become bone themselves.

Child's bone - growth takes place throughout

Growth plates

Adolescent's bone - growth only at growth plates

Adult bone - no more growth

A baby grows most in the first year of life.

By the age of 2, a child is roughly half its adult height.

Most children grow an average of 5-7.5cm (2-3in) a year.

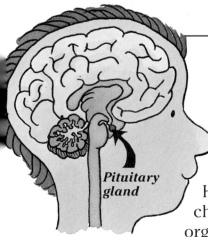

GROWTH CONTROL

When and how much you grow is controlled by hormones. Hormones are chemicals released by organs in your body, called glands. They carry instructions to your cells, telling them what to do. Growth hormones are produced by a gland in your brain called the pituitary gland.

At puberty, when a child becomes sexually mature, sex hormones are also released. These lead to a growth spurt. They also lead to changes in the skeleton which are different for men and women.

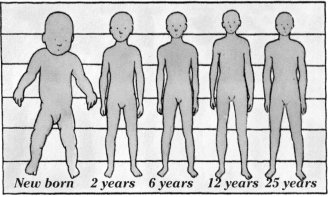

Pituitary gland

New born   2 years   6 years   12 years 25 years

Different parts of your body grow at different ages. This chart shows how your body proportions change as you grow up.

Female sex hormones, called estrogens, make a woman's pelvis grow wider to make it easier for her to have children. The male sex hormone, testosterone, causes men's bones to grow larger and heavier than women's.

CRUMBLY BONES

Sex hormones also make sure your bones repair themselves and absorb enough minerals to keep them strong. Old people produce fewer sex hormones, which means their bones are weaker. This can lead to a disease called osteoporosis, which makes bones crumbly, fragile and more breakable.

Most girls start puberty between the ages of 10 to 14. (Boys between 12 to 16.) It lasts for about 3-4 years, until maturity is reached.

Old people may stoop as their bones get weaker.

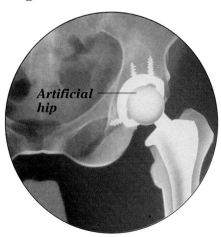

Artificial hip

People can have an operation to replace a weak hip with an artificial one.

For links to websites where you can do a fun activity to see how people's faces change as they grow older and find out more about how bones grow, go to **www.usborne-quicklinks.com**

BROKEN BONES

Although your bones are strong, they can break if you put too much weight on them or twist a joint the wrong way. Broken bones are called fractures. Some fractures are more serious than others.

Girl having an arm x-ray

X-RAYS

If doctors suspect you have a fracture, they take an x-ray. An x-ray machine sends a beam of rays through your body. The rays pass through your skin, fat and muscle to a special photographic plate, which turns dark. But the rays cannot pass through your bones, so your bones show up on the plate as light areas. From this, doctors can tell if you have a fracture and how serious it is.

The x-rays on the right show different types of fractures. They are tinted to make them clearer.

Simple fracture - bone is broken completely in two.

Compound fracture - part of broken bone pokes out of the skin.

To help a bone repair itself, doctors use plaster casts to keep the pieces of bone in place.

26

For links to websites where you can see x-rays of lots of bones and try an activity about broken bones, go to **www.usborne-quicklinks.com**

MENDING BONES

With a bit of help from doctors, your bones will mend themselves, but it can take several months. This is a long time compared with how long it takes your skin to heal. It only takes a few days for new skin to grow over a cut.

Very bad fractures may need to be pinned together with metal pins. These can set off metal detectors at airports.

A bone mends itself in three stages:

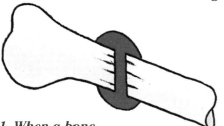

1. When a bone fractures, blood vessels are broken too. Blood pours from the torn vessels and forms a clot, around the broken ends of bone.

2. New bone cells move into the blood clot. As more bone cells are made, the blood clot is gradually replaced by bone.

3. Any old pieces of broken bone which jut out are absorbed into the blood stream, so the repair is smoothed down.

BONE MARROW DISEASE

Leukemia is a disease of the bone marrow. It upsets the production of healthy white blood cells. These are the very cells that fight disease. There are several different types of leukemia. In one type, the marrow produces too many white blood cells, so the red ones are swamped. In another, white blood cells are let into the blood too early, before they are ready to carry out their disease-killing tasks. In a third type, the body is overrun with useless old white blood cells which should have died.

No one knows exactly what causes leukemia, but most cases can be treated with drugs or radiotherapy. In radiotherapy the problem white blood cells are zapped with high doses of x-rays in order to kill them. Many patients make a full recovery.

A leukemia patient. The drugs that treat leukemia may make your hair fall out, but they can cure the disease completely.

MUSCLE TROUBLE

Muscles often cause aches and pains, but this is usually nothing serious. You may have "pulled" a muscle by making it stretch too violently or unexpectedly, or strained muscles which don't usually have to work hard. Rest and a relaxing hot bath are often the best things for this sort of muscle pain. There are, however, more serious things that can go wrong with your muscles.

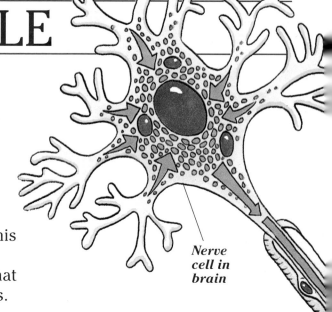

Nerve cell in brain

DYSTROPHIES

Inside all your cells are chains of chemicals called genes. Genes carry instructions which tell your cells what to do. Particular genes in your muscle cells are essential for your muscles to contract. In some people these genes are faulty and they suffer from diseases called muscular dystrophies. Their muscles gradually stop working and waste away. Most sufferers end up in a wheelchair and many die at a young age.

At the moment there is no cure for dystrophies. Scientists are hoping that one day they may be able to correct bad genes or replace them with healthy ones. But this is still a long way in the future.

Scientists need very strong microscopes to study genes.

PARALYSIS

Muscles contract when they receive messages from the brain. So, if someone damages their brain, or the nerves which connect it to the rest of their body, this can also affect their muscles. They could suffer paralysis and be unable to move their muscles.

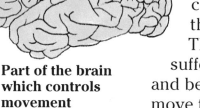

Part of the brain which controls movement

Brain damage is not necessarily permanent. Sometimes patients regain feeling and movement in parts of their bodies. Doctors don't really know fully how the brain works, so no one understands quite how or why this happens.

It's very important to wear a helmet when you are cycling so your head is protected if you fall off.

For a link to a website where you can find lots of exercise tips and online activities, go to www.usborne-quicklinks.com

MYELIN AND MULTIPLE SCLEROSIS

Messages, or impulses, from your brain travel to your muscles via nerve cells. These nerve cells are covered with a layer of fat, called a myelin sheath. In a disease called multiple sclerosis (MS), these fatty layers are destroyed. Without their myelin sheaths, the nerve cells can't transmit messages properly.

This means the messages that reach the muscles are not as clear and strong as they should be. So sufferers gradually lose the use of their muscles. No one has yet discovered the cause of MS. Doctors have come up with theories linking it to climate, diet, genes and viruses, but none of them has been proved. Although some of the symptoms of MS can be treated with drugs there is no actual cure.

This diagram shows a nerve cell damaged by multiple sclerosis.

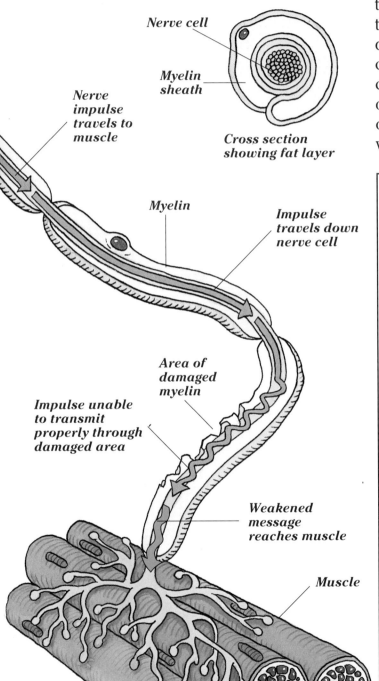

Nerve cell

Myelin sheath

Cross section showing fat layer

Nerve impulse travels to muscle

Myelin

Impulse travels down nerve cell

Area of damaged myelin

Impulse unable to transmit properly through damaged area

Weakened message reaches muscle

Muscle

PHYSIOTHERAPY

If muscles are not used, they very quickly become flabby and weak. So, if, for example, you have been ill in bed for a long time, you will need to do special exercises to build up your strength gradually. These are called physiotherapy. There are many different types of physiotherapy, such as massage, heat treatment and swimming.

PREHISTORIC BONES

E volution is the theory that living things have changed, or evolved, over millions of years. Many scientists believe that the animals that live on the earth today are descended from simpler forms that lived in earlier ages. Much of the evidence for evolution lies in the fossils of old bones, some many millions of years old.

BURYING THE EVIDENCE

Fossils are the remains of animals or plants which have been turned into rock. Bones are fossilized when they are covered with mud or sand which, over millions of years, is compressed to form rock. Tiny rock particles enter the bones which become fossils.

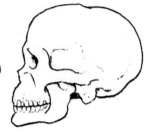

Ramapithecus – ape living 12 million years ago. First apes to leave trees.

Australopithecus afarensis – ape living 4–3 million years ago. First apes to use sticks and stones.

Homo habilis (handy human) – living 2–1.5 million years ago. First to make tools.

HUMAN EVOLUTION

Scientists have found very few fossils of the ancestors of human beings. But they have built up a picture of how they think humans evolved, based on skulls and teeth which have been unearthed. As new evidence is discovered, new theories of human evolution are put forward.

Homo erectus (upright human) – living 1.6 million–400,000 years ago, probably spread from Africa to Europe. First to use fire.

Homo sapiens sapiens - first modern human, evolved 100,000 years ago.

This time line shows how humans may have evolved.

These skulls show how the shape of our heads has changed over millions of years.

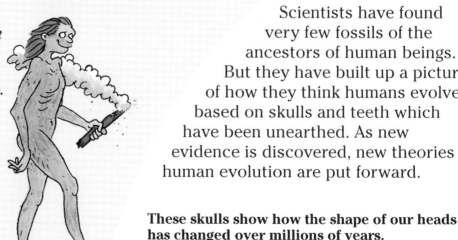

Skull of Australopithecus

Skull of Homo erectus

Skull of modern human

AMAZING FACTS

Robert Wadlow with his brother

The largest recorded human bone belonged to a German giant called Constantine. His femur was 76cm (29.9in) long.

Giantism and dwarfism are medical conditions. They are caused when the pituitary gland, which makes growth hormones, malfunctions.

The strongest muscle in your body is the jaw muscle which you use for biting.

The tallest recorded man in the world ever was Robert Wadlow. He was born in 1918 and died aged 22, measuring 272cm (8ft 11.1in). He hadn't reached his full height when he died and doctors think he could have grown to 274cm (9ft).

The muscle with the longest name is the *levator labii superioris alaeque nasi*. This is Latin. The muscle is in your face and it enables you to curl your upper lip and twitch your nose.

The most active muscles in your body are your eye muscles. They contract about 100,000 times a day. Much of this movement takes place when you are dreaming and your eyes flicker under your closed eyelids.

Elvis Presley – one of the world's most famous lip curlers

Gosh!

That is short!

Told you.

Gul Mohammed

The shortest recorded fully-grown man in the world is the dwarf Gul Mohammed of New Delhi, India. He was measured in 1990 and was only 57cm (22½in) tall.

The largest muscle in your body is in your bottom. But, in pregnant women, the muscular womb (where a new baby grows) can grow bigger than the bottom.

Your smallest muscle is less than 0.127cm (0.05in) long. It is attached to a tiny bone in your ear.

QUIZ ANSWERS

Page 4
    The same number- 7!

Page 18
    1. Maximum strength
    2. Specific strength and endurance
    3. Explosive strength

Page 20
    4, 5, 6, 7 and 8

For links to websites where you can compare ancient and modern human bones, and find fun body quizzes and activities to print out, go to **www.usborne-quicklinks.com**

Achilles heel, 7
Achilles tendon, 7
aerobic respiration, 16, 17
anaerobic respiration, 16, 17
archeologists, 13
arthritis, 9
ATP, 16, 17

biceps, 6, 10
blood, 6, 12, 14-15, 16, 20, 27
bone,
    biggest in body, 5
    biggest recorded, 31
    broken, 26-27
    cells, 3, 12, 24, 27
    compact, 12
    joints, 8-9, 26
    marrow, 12, 27
    smallest in body, 4
    spongy, 12
    tissue, 3, 12
brain, 3, 4, 10, 11, 14, 20, 21, 25,
    28
breathing, 16, 20

calcium, 12, 13
cartilage, 8, 9, 24
cells, 3, 10, 11, 12, 13, 16, 21, 24,
    27, 28, 29
contracting, 10, 11, 13, 18, 19
coordination, 3

diaphragm, 20, 22
digestive system, 20
dwarfism, 31

evolution, 5, 30
exercise, 9, 19
exoskeleton, 5
eye, 21, 31

fossils, 30

fractures, 26, 27

giantism, 31
growing, 24-25

heart, 4, 14-15, 16, 17
hormones, 25

invertebrates, 5
involuntary actions, 11, 20, 21
involuntary muscles, 20-21

joints, 8-9, 26

lactic acid, 17
larynx, 22
leukemia, 27
ligaments, 8, 9
lungs, 4, 14, 15, 16, 20, 22

marrow, 12, 27
movement, 3, 6, 9, 10-11, 17, 18
multiple sclerosis, 29
muscle,
    biggest in body , 31
    cells, 3, 13, 16
    digestive, 20
    fatigue, 6, 17
    hand, 2
    heart, 13, 14-15
    involuntary, 20-21
    most active, 31
    skeletal, 6, 10, 13
    smallest in body, 31
    smooth, 13
    stomach, 6, 20
    striped, 13
    strongest, 31
    tissue, 3, 13
    voluntary, 6
muscular dystrophies, 28

nerves, 10, 11, 12, 21, 28, 29

ossification, 24
osteoarthritis, 9
osteologists, 3
osteopaths, 3
osteoporosis, 25
oxygen, 6, 15, 16, 17

paralysis, 28
physiotherapy, 3, 29
pulse, 15

reflex actions, 11
respiration, 16-17
rheumatoid arthritis, 9

skeletal muscles, 6, 10, 13
skeleton, 4-5, 6, 13, 24
skull, 4, 21, 30
speech, 22-23
sphincters, 20
spinal cord, 10, 11
spine, 4, 5
sports, 18-19
strength, 18-19
synovial fluid, 8, 9
synovial membrane, 8

tendons, 7, 9
tissue, 3, 13
tongue, 23
training, 19
triceps, 6, 10

vertebrates, 5
vocal cords, 22, 23
voice box, 22, 23
voluntary actions, 11
voluntary muscles, 6

x-rays, 26, 27

ACKNOWLEDGEMENTS
Page 3: Bone tissue, Michael Abbey/Science Photo Library
(SPL). Page 7: ©Usborne Publishing Ltd. Photography by
Howard Allman. Page 9: CNRI/SPL. Page 10: Don Fawcett/SPL.
Page 11: Anatomical studies, The Royal Collection©,
Her Majesty Queen Elizabeth II. Page 13: Photo: Museum
of London Archaeology Service. Page 14: John Radcliffe
Hospital/SPL. Page 18: Gray Mortimer/Allsport. Page 25:
Chris Bjornberg/SPL. Page 26: Radiographer - Will and Deni
Mcintyre/SPL; Simple fracture - SPL; Compound fracture -
SPL. Page 27: Simon Fraser/Royal Victoria
Infirmary/Newcastle/SPL. Cover: Alfred Pasieka/SPL.

Usborne Publishing is not responsible, and does not accept liability, for the
availability or content of any website other than its own, or for any exposure to
harmful, offensive, or inaccurate material which may appear on the Web. Usborne
Publishing will have no liability for any damage or loss caused by viruses that may
be down loaded as a result of browsing the sites we recommend.

First published in 1997 by Usborne Publishing Ltd,
83–85 Saffron Hill, London EC1N 8RT, England. www.usborne.com
Copyright © 2004, 1997 Usborne Publishing Ltd.

All rights reserved. No part of this publication may be reproduced, stored in a
retrieval system, or transmitted in any form or by any means, electronic, mechanical,
photocopying, recording or otherwise, without the prior permission of the publisher.
The name Usborne and the devices ⚲ ⊜ are Trade Marks of Usborne Publishing Ltd.
Printed in Spain. UE. This edition published in America in 2004.